BACKGROUND FOR THE HISTORICAL NOVEL

A historical novel is one in which fictional characters live in a historic period. Characters may be based closely or loosely upon accounts of those who had lived then. Authors take varying degrees of poetic license with this form of literature.

The appeal of a historical novel is that it offers the reader a more immediate sense of history than does a textbook. Characters, conflicts, and events seem to come alive in the authentic atmosphere of the period. Settings, themes, plot elements and structure, language, dialogue — all of these components of fiction are derived, with varying degrees of artistic license, from documented historical information. The drawback of this form of literature, however, is that an author may change historical reality to fit the purposes of the narrative. It may be difficult to determine the author's sources of information. For that reason, it is important to approach any historical novel with some understanding of the times about which it was written.

The Witch of Blackbird Pond is historically accurate for the most part. Most of the characters are fictional, but the framework is based on history. Documented historical individuals and events do figure in the story. How would an author research a historical period prior to writing a novel? Where can historical information be found?

As you read, notice the historical details embedded within the story and check the information in non-fiction sources such as history textbooks, encyclopedias, and biographies. The book will thus enrich your understanding of colonial New England.

PRE-READING VOCABULARY

Words that Reflect Colonial Times

This is a list of words that were common during colonial times. The author uses them in order to make the novel seem more authentic as historical fiction. Discuss these words and their meanings.

Goodwife ("Goody")	masque
pillory	tryst
stocks	stout (noun)
dame school	selectman
the common	hornbook

Nautical Pursuits

Since much of this novel involves the sea, there are many nautical terms the reader needs to know. Definitions of the following important terms should be found in the dictionary.

brigantine	aft
rigging	tack
capstan	cross-staff
prow	

PRE-READING ACTIVITY

This is a list of ways in which most people in colonial Connecticut spent their time. How was each of these activities performed? How has each activity changed over 200 years?

1. farming by hand
2. making clothing
3. making soap and candles
4. cleaning the house
5. preparing food
6. building a home
7. attending church meeting

CHAPTER 1

Vocabulary: Draw a line from each word on the left to its definition on the right.

1. embark
2. disembark
3. nonchalance
4. hostile
5. heathen
6. retching
7. repulse
8. dour
9. daft

10. clergyman
11. sodden

a. foolish, insane
b. unfriendly, angry
c. priest, minister, or rabbi
d. vomiting
e. to begin activities, to board a ship
f. soaked
g. to drive back, to disgust
h. having confidence and an easy manner
i. person who does not believe in the Jewish, Christian, or Muslim God
j. stern, severe
k. to get off a ship, to land

Activity: In the opening chapter of a book the author sets the stage for the story. On page 1 of this novel the author gives us a great deal of background information. Read this page to find out:

1. WHO is the story about?

2. WHAT is happening?

3. WHERE is it taking place?

4. WHEN does the action occur?

5. WHY is it happening?

   (You have probably realized that page 1 does not answer the WHY question. Read the remainder of the chapter to find out why Kit is on the Dolphin.)

Questions:

1. Why is Kit making the journey to Connecticut?

2. What were Kit's first impressions of America? What does this reveal about her background and character?

3. How did the people aboard the boat react when Kit rescued the doll? Focus on the reactions of Nat, John, and Goodwife Cruff.

4. What are Kit's views regarding Puritans? Cite evidence from Chapter 1 to defend your answer.

Prediction: It is clear that Kit is the central character in the book. What do we know about her family background, attitudes, and temperament? How do you think all of these attributes will affect Kit's future in the Connecticut Colony?

CHAPTER 2

Vocabulary: Draw a line from each word on the left to its definition on the right. Then choose one of the vocabulary words to complete each of the following sentences.

1. daub
2. endure
3. furtively
4. frank
5. intangible
6. punctilious
7. theology
8. squall
9. tanner

a. outspoken, honest
b. strict in observing good manners
c. a sudden severe storm
d. to smear, to paint badly
e. someone who makes hides into leather
f. not able to be touched, abstract
g. to last, to continue, to bear
h. the study of religion
i. quickly and secretly

. . . .

1. A _____ at sea can cause small boats to capsize.

2. I need your _____ opinion about my new dress.

3. Many people _____ the cold weather during a football game in order to see their favorite team play.

4. The thief glanced _____ in the direction of the policeman in the hope that he had not been noticed.

Questions:

1. What new information does Kit reveal about her background?

2. What does John tell Kit about himself?

3. Nat says: "But we Eatons, we're mighty proud that our ship has a good honest stink of horses!" How does this statement reflect Nat's attitude toward slavery? How does it contrast with Kit's attitude?

4. What do you think Kit learned from her discussion with Nat on the subject of slavery?

A Cliffhanger:

Writers often build suspense into their stories by introducing a surprise element at the end of a chapter. It encourages you to read on in order to find out what will happen next.

What is the "cliffhanger" in this chapter?

What effect will this surprise have on the other characters in the story?

What more has this taught us about Kit's personality?

CHAPTERS 3 AND 4

Vocabulary: Draw a line from each word on the left to its definition on the right.

1. nondescript	a. that which is vain or useless
2. ponder	b. skillful, skilled in use of the hands
3. concede	c. thin cereal
4. vanity	d. to think about carefully
5. gaudy	e. polished
6. deft	f. showy and in bad taste
7. burnished	g. of no recognized type
8. grotesque	h. odd or unnatural in shape
9. quaver	i. to admit to be true
10. gruel	j. tremble

Questions:

1. What did Kit think about the town of Wethersfield on the day of her arrival?

2. What kind of reception did Kit receive from Uncle Matthew, Aunt Rachel, Judith and Mercy?

3. What effect did Kit's trunks have upon her family? What contrast did this reveal between her accustomed life and that of her relatives?

4. Kit gives a gift to each of the women in the Wood family. How does each gift reflect the character of the person to whom it is given?

5. What was there about the Wood household that surprised Kit on that first day in Wethersfield?

6. Judith remarks: "If we had to have a cousin at all, why couldn't it have been a boy?" What is the importance of this question, and how does it reflect the times?

Writing Activity:

In the late seventeenth century, an educated person such as Kit often kept a diary of daily activities. Imagine you are Kit and you wish to record your first impressions of your new home. Write a diary entry that includes information about Wethersfield, the Wood family, and life in Connecticut Colony.

CHAPTERS 5, 6, AND 7

Vocabulary: It is often possible to determine the meaning of unfamiliar words from their context. Consider the underlined word in each of the following passages and choose the most appropriate meaning.

1. The modish bonnet with curling white feathers seemed to her uncle a crowning <u>affront</u>. "You will mock the Lord's assembly."

   a. compliment   b. insult   c. hat   d. treat

2. The deacons' wives were surveying her from feathered hat to slippered toe. She did not look like a <u>pauper</u>.

   a. angry person   b. rich person   c. poor person   d. silly person

3. Most of the churchgoers did not come near her. She glimpsed Goodwife Cruff, surrounded by a close huddle of women, all darting <u>venomous</u> glances in Kit's direction.

   a. pleasant   b. spiteful   c. loving   d. weary

4. The brick oven had been heated for two nights in a row, and the whole family had gone without sugar since Sunday to make sure that the minister's <u>notorious</u> sweet tooth would be satisfied.

   a. well-known   b. ancient   c. sickly   d. unknown

5. Reverend Bulkely smiled whenever he looked at Kit. But the greatest part of his <u>condescension</u> he had bestowed on Kit, once he had understood that her grandfather had been Sir Francis Tyler.

   a. guilt   b. unpleasant behavior   c. patronizing behavior   d. instruction

6. John's voice was low-pitched but clear, and the words fell with a musical <u>cadence</u> that was a delight.

   a. ability   b. odor   c. sight   d. rhythm

Questions:

1. Both Judith and Matthew do not want Kit to wear her silk dress to meeting. Their reasons are different. Explain.

2. As Kit walks to meeting, she observes several things that are strange to her. She notices the sabbath houses, the pillory, the stocks, the whipping post, and the meeting house standing alone in the clearing. What does each of these things tell us about life in Wethersfield?

3. At the meeting, what impression did Kit make upon the townspeople and William?

4. At dinner, Matthew responds to Dr. Bulkely by saying, "Do you think we have labored and sacrificed all these years to build up a free government only to hand it over [to Andros] now without a murmur?" What does this mean? What does it tell us about Matthew Wood?

Chapters 5, 6, and 7 (cont.)

5. How does Dr. Bulkely present the Royalist point of view?

6. What is the relationship between William "making up his mind" and the construction of his house?

7. Describe what happens when William first "comes to call" on Kit.

8. When John and William come to visit, the men and women are each concerned with different issues. What concerns the men? What concerns the women? What does this tell us about the times?

Writing Activity: "A Penny for Your Thoughts, William Ashby"

Although William hardly spoke during his evening with Kit, many thoughts must have been going through his mind. Write what his thoughts might have been regarding Kit, her family, and the future.

CHAPTERS 8 AND 9

Vocabulary: Draw a line from each word on the left to its definition on the right.

1. menial		a. extremely hungry
2. precarious		b. permitted, approved
3. sober		c. calmness, tranquility
4. ravenous		d. proper behavior
5. composure		e. pertaining to domestic servants
6. obstreperous		f. to move in an idle manner
7. sanctioned		g. bent and twisted
8. decorum		h. serious, not drunk
9. loiter		i. noisy, unruly
10. gnarled		j. uncertain, unreliable

Questions:

1. Why does Judith think that Hannah Tupper is like a witch?

2. What is the connection between Kit's weeding onions and her marrying William?

3. What "more immediate escape offered itself [to Kit] that very noontime"?

4. How does the prospect of teaching make Kit feel about herself?

5. What does Mercy reveal about the history of the Wood family that helps us to understand Matthew Wood?

6. Describe the dame school — its teachers, educational materials, location, and discipline.

7. How did Kit's innocence and creativity lead to the loss of her job?

8. What is there about Hannah that differs sharply from Judith's description of her?

Prediction:

There is another cliffhanger at the end of Chapter 9. Kit "walked up the path to a square frame house, and knocked boldly on the door of Mr. Eleazer Kimberly." What do you predict will be the result of this visit?

Writing Activity:

Kit went to the meadow when she was feeling ashamed and sorrowful. Do you have a special place where you go when you are sad? Write a description of your special place and tell about one time when you went there.

CHAPTERS 10, 11 AND 12

Vocabulary: Use a thesaurus to find a synonym for each of the words below. Then use all of the given words in an original paragraph.

1. malicious _____
2. diligent _____
3. revoke _____

4. docile _____
5. morose _____
6. adroit _____

_____

_____

_____

_____

_____

_____

_____

Questions:

1. Why was Kit unable to promise that she would not return to Hannah's house?

2. How did Kit know that Judith was in love?

3. What hardships did Hannah endure in Wethersfield because she was a Quaker?

4. What did Nat and Kit have in common?

5. Why didn't Prudence attend school with the other children?

6. What does the gift of leftover apple tart reveal about Aunt Rachel's character?

7. What does Nat mean when he says to Kit, "I can still see the green feathers if I look hard enough. But they've done their best to make you into a sparrow, haven't they"?

8. What political opinions do Nat and Uncle Matthew share?

9. Why was Kit embarrassed when she returned from Hannah's house?

10. How does the reader become aware of the change of seasons? How does this change affect the Wood family?

Chapters 10, 11, and 12 (cont.)

Activity: "Love's Great Mystery"

List all of the single young people in Wethersfield:

Young Men   Young Women

_____   _____

_____   _____

_____   _____

Years ago, it was customary to carve the initials of your beloved on a tree stump. Imagine that these three hearts were found on a tree in Wethersfield. From what you know of our main characters, complete the hearts.

Give your reasons for pairing each of these couples:

1.

2.

3.

CHAPTERS 13 AND 14

Vocabulary: Draw a line from each word on the left to its definition on the right.

1. propitious
2. infatuated
3. foreboding
4. jubilant
5. brazen
6. perplexed
7. resolute

a. blindly in love, foolishly in love
b. insolent, defiant
c. puzzled
d. prediction of evil
e. determined
f. favorable
g. showing great joy

Questions:

1. When John says, "There is something I want to speak to your father about," only the reader knows what he means. Each character interprets this through his or her limited understanding of the situation. Tell how each of the following characters interprets John's statement:

   Judith   John   Uncle Matthew
   Kit   Mercy   Aunt Rachel

2. What tragedy was caused by this misunderstanding?

3. William informs Kit that he would like to speak to her Uncle Matthew. What is Kit's reaction?

4. What effect could Sir Edmund Andros' arrival have upon the Wood family, as well as the entire Connecticut Colony?

Activity:

Although Kit has "long since decided what her answer would be" to William, she still has mixed feelings about her future with him. List reasons for and against Kit marrying William.

For William	*Against William*

CLOZE ACTIVITY:

The following passage tells about witchcraft in the Connecticut Colony. Read the entire passage once without filling in the blanks. During a second reading, use the context to replace the missing words. There is a word choice at the bottom of the page if needed.

These were the years when people became obsessed by a fear of witchcraft. They believed a _____ [1] could sell his soul to the devil _____ [2] would then have the power to do _____ [3] sorts of mischief. A particular wave of _____ [4] swept across New England in the 1680's _____ [5] 1690's. When anything unusual happened — when a _____ [6] became ill, or butter would not churn, _____ [7] a cow died unexpectedly — people looked for _____ [8] witch who was responsible.

Any odd or _____ [9] old woman might be suspected. Sometimes suspicion _____ [10] on a young woman of whom the _____ [11] was distrustful. Some women became hysterical _____ [12] accused and confessed to all sorts of _____ [13] things. Some denied everything. It really made _____ [14] difference when the witch-hunting fever struck. There _____ [15] trials, presided over by ministers and magistrates. _____ [16] were tests. Sometimes an accused witch was _____ [17] into the water. If she floated she _____ [18] guilty. If she drowned, she was innocent, _____ [19] judgment was not much use to _____ [20] any longer. Those whom the juries found guilty without the water test were generally hanged.

Word Choice:

her	was	unlikely	fell
child	terror	town	which
there	little	the	and
person	all	thrown	were
when	eccentric	or	and

BACKGROUND INFORMATION

The Connecticut Charter:

Here is a historical account concerning the Connecticut Charter. Although it is derived from history texts, it is not clear how much is absolute fact and how much is myth. Compare this account to the one offered in the novel. How are they the same? How are they different?

The hour being late, Governor Andros asked Governor Treat and the Connecticut representatives to join him for dinner at the inn. After dinner it was suggested that Andros and the Connecticut men hold their conference in an upstairs room of the inn. Two candelabra, holding fourteen candles, were brought for light. The meeting began. Andros spoke quietly but ended by demanding the charter. Governor Treat spoke about what the charter meant to Connecticut, but finally he had to produce it.

He snipped the deerskin thong that held the rolled parchment. The document half unrolled itself across the table. There was some more talk about how precious it was to Connecticut and how much effort, blood and money had gone into achieving it. One of the older representatives, a man named Andrew Leete, who had been ill for some time, got up to speak. He talked with growing emotion. Then suddenly, he fell forward across the table, unconscious. As he fell, his arms knocked over both candelabra and all the candles were extinguished. The room was in darkness.

By the time the candles were lighted again the charter was gone. According to legend, the charter had been handed, under cover of the darkness, to a young captain of the militia who was standing next to a bay window. This young man, Joseph Wadsworth, stepped quickly through the open window, onto the stairs outside it and then ran down them and into the night. He evaded the English soldiers of Sir Edmund's guard, crossed the little "riveret" that ran through the town just there and made his way to the home of Samuel Wyllys, one of the original guardians of the charter.

A great oak tree stood in front of the Wyllys house. It was the same oak that the Dutch captain Adrian Block had seen when he sailed up the Connecticut River in 1614. It was the oak under which the Suckiaug Indians had smoked their peace pipes, the oak that signaled the time to plant corn when its leaves were the size of a mouse's ear.

The tree was old now, and there was a hollow in it. Captain Wadsworth took off his soldier's tunic, wrapped it around the charter and thrust the package deep into the hollow of the great oak. Then he ran off into the darkness.

Back at the inn, Sir Edmund did not allow himself any bad temper when it was seen that the charter was gone. He had come to force Connecticut men into a position where they must either surrender their charter or resist the king openly. He had failed in both goals. The charter was gone. The Connecticut leaders had not resisted him.

CHAPTERS 15 AND 16

Vocabulary: Draw a line from each word on the left to its definition on the right.

1. commonwealth
2. chagrin
3. insubordination
4. elated
5. constable
6. blasphemy
7. retribution
8. premonition
9. reconcile

a. an act of being disobedient
b. cursing
c. a feeling of fear about a future event
d. retaliation
e. to settle an argument
f. an officer of the peace
g. annoyance, shame
h. very happy, overjoyed
i. a group of states linked together by choice

Questions:

1. Why has William changed his political views?

2. Why are so many of the men in Wethersfield angered about the appointment of a governor who represents the crown?

3. How was Governor Andros received by the the people of Wethersfield?

4. A symbol is an object which stands for an idea. For example: the flag is a symbol of our country. What does the charter symbolize to the people of Connecticut? Why is it so important to keep it safe until "hard times have passed"?

5. Kit has "understood for the first time what her Aunt had seen in that fierce man to make her cross an ocean at his side." What has Kit come to realize about Uncle Matthew?

6. How did Nat display his dislike for William Ashby? Do you think the punishment for this deed was appropriate?

7. What are the advantages and disadvantages for Prudence in studying with Kit at Hannah's house?

8. What news do we learn about John? What reasons are given for his departure? Could there be another reason for his leaving?

CHAPTERS 17 AND 18

Vocabulary: Draw a line from each word on the left to its definition on the right.

1. mope
2. malady
3. vigil
4. infidel
5. slander
6. serenity
7. haggard
8. inveigle

a. a person without religious belief
b. calmness
c. to be in poor spirits, to be sad
d. to persuade by flattery
e. a watch or guard
f. false, evil statements
g. looking tired and worn
h. sickness

Questions:

1. How did illness in the Wood family affect Kit?

2. Why did Matthew Wood and Dr. Bulkely suspend their feud?

3. Why have the people of Wethersfield waited until the time of the epidemic to accuse Hannah of witchcraft openly?

4. How did Hannah escape from the townspeople?

5. What reason does Kit give for not leaving with Nat? What does this reveal to us about Kit's changing character?

6. Why have Matthew's feelings changed toward Kit?

7. What was found in Hannah's house that incriminated Kit?

8. How did Matthew feel Kit should be punished?

9. Why is this the first time Kit feels guilty about her association with Hannah and Prudence?

10. What punishments does the constable describe for former witches?

Writing Activity:

After her sleepless night in the shed, how do you think Kit appeared to the townspeople? How could her appearance affect the inquiry? Express your answer in two well-written paragraphs.

CHAPTER 19

Vocabulary: Use a dictionary to find the definitions of each of the following words. Then use each of these words to fill in the blanks in the sentences below.

1. instigate _____

2. alleged _____

3. vehement _____

4. pandemonium _____

5. intercede _____

· ·

1. The _____ killer was brought to trial for murder.

2. If you _____ bad behavior in others, you are just as guilty as those who misbehave.

3. There was _____ in the classroom as soon as the teacher walked out the door.

4. An arbitrator was hired to _____ between the striking workers and management.

5. The child was _____ in her cries for a balloon.

Questions:

1. Describe and comment upon the various accusations made against Kit.

2. Both Matthew and Dr. Bulkely testify in Kit's defense. What approach does each man use?

3. How can a copybook serve as further evidence of Kit's witchcraft?

4. Explain how Nat "saves the day" with his mystery witness.

5. How do you think this incident could change Prudence's life?

Activity:

Re-enact the courtroom scene, using the actual conversation in Chapter 19 as the script. Assign the parts of:

Kit	Goodwife Cruff
Matthew Wood	Goodman Cruff
Prudence	Captain Talcott
Dr. Bulkely	Clerk

CHAPTERS 20 AND 21

Vocabulary: Draw a line from each word on the left to its definition on the right.

1. slackened
2. surreptitiously
3. conceded
4. waver
5. concoct
6. perpetual
7. arduous
8. spinster
9. abate
10. hoard
11. recede
12. amend

a. difficult
b. change
c. make, mix
d. save
e. secretly
f. sway
g. lessened
h. unmarried woman
i. admitted
j. go back
k. always
l. let up

Questions:

1. What were Kit's feelings about the first snowfall?

2. What was the nature of Kit's final conversation with William?

3. What happened to John Holbrook which worried everyone?

4. Why does Kit come to hate the New England winter? What decision does she make?

5. What thoughts does Kit have when she walks to the meadow?

6. What was Kit "waiting for" when she "found a way to meet every trading ship that came up the river"?

7. Who arrived in May?

8. What is the significance of the name of Nat's new ketch?

9. What did Kit and the ketch have to wait for?

Writing Activity:

In one paragraph give your reasons for liking or disliking the author's ending to the novel.

POST-READING ACTIVITIES:

1. Locate pictures of early New England colonies in the library. If you are artistic, you can sketch pictures of a pillory, the stocks, a meeting house, a church, a typical home.

2. Make a list of all of the tasks that might be needed to make a simple New England dinner.

   For example: chopping wood

   churning butter

3. Contrast colonial life with present-day life. Some aspects that may be considered are:

   religious observance

   clothing

   dating etiquette

   social life

   education

4. In times past a young girl would bring to her marriage a dowry of items to launch her wedded life. They were usually stored in a hope chest until after the wedding. What should a girl like Kit or Judith collect in her hope chest? If you would prefer to take a male point of view, what would Nat or William be most likely to take along to a new home?

5. Imagine that you find yourself in a situation like Kit's. Completely alone, you must decide upon a destination. Where would you go? Would you inform anyone of your plans? What might life be like when you got there? Write a brief story about yourself in this hypothetical situation.

SUGGESTIONS FOR FURTHER READING

Avi. *Encounter at Easton*. Pantheon.

*   *The Fighting Ground*. Harper and Row.

     Night Journey. Pantheon.

Clapp, Patricia. *Constance: A Story of Early Plymouth*. Lothrop.

* Collier, James Lincoln and Collier, Christopher. *My Brother Sam is Dead*. Scholastic.

Fast, Howard. *April Morning*. Bantam.

     The Hessian. Bantam.

Finlayson, Ann. *Rebecca's War*. Dell.

* Forbes, Esther. *Johnny Tremain*. Dell.

     A Mirror for Witches. Dell.

O'Dell, Scott. *Sarah Bishop*. Houghton Mifflin.

Petry, Ann. *Tituba of Salem Village*. T.Y. Crowell.

Quackenbush, Robert. *The House on Stink Alley*. Dell.

*   NOVEL-TIES Study Guides are available for these titles.